T0024873

TRENDS IN SOUTHEAST ASIA

The **ISEAS – Yusof Ishak Institute** (formerly Institute of Southeast Asian Studies) is an autonomous organization established in 1968. It is a regional centre dedicated to the study of socio-political, security, and economic trends and developments in Southeast Asia and its wider geostrategic and economic environment. The Institute's research programmes are grouped under Regional Economic Studies (RES), Regional Strategic and Political Studies (RSPS), and Regional Social and Cultural Studies (RSCS). The Institute is also home to the ASEAN Studies Centre (ASC), the Singapore APEC Study Centre and the Temasek History Research Centre (THRC).

ISEAS Publishing, an established academic press, has issued more than 2,000 books and journals. It is the largest scholarly publisher of research about Southeast Asia from within the region. ISEAS Publishing works with many other academic and trade publishers and distributors to disseminate important research and analyses from and about Southeast Asia to the rest of the world.

THE UNREALIZED MAHATHIR-ANWAR TRANSITIONS

Social Divides and Political Consequences

Khoo Boo Teik

ISSUE
15
2021

 YUSOF ISHAK INSTITUTE

Published by: ISEAS Publishing
                  30 Heng Mui Keng Terrace
                  Singapore 119614
                  publish@iseas.edu.sg
                  http://bookshop.iseas.edu.sg

The author is wholly responsible for the views expressed in this book which do not necessarily reflect those of the publisher.

ISEAS Library Cataloguing-in-Publication Data

Name(s): Khoo, Boo Teik, 1955-, author.
Title: The unrealized Mahathir-Anwar transitions : social divides and political consequences / by Khoo Boo Teik.
Description: Singapore : ISEAS–Yusof Ishak Institute, July 2021. | Series: Trends in Southeast Asia, ISSN 0219-3213 ; TRS15/21 | Includes bibliographical references.
Identifiers: ISBN 9789815011005 (soft cover) | ISBN 9789815011012 (pdf)
Subjects: LCSH: Malaysia—Politics and government. | Malaysia—Social conditions.
Classification: LCC DS501 I59T no. 15(2021)

Typeset by Superskill Graphics Pte Ltd
Printed in Singapore by Mainland Press Pte Ltd

FOREWORD

The economic, political, strategic and cultural dynamism in Southeast Asia has gained added relevance in recent years with the spectacular rise of giant economies in East and South Asia. This has drawn greater attention to the region and to the enhanced role it now plays in international relations and global economics.

The sustained effort made by Southeast Asian nations since 1967 towards a peaceful and gradual integration of their economies has had indubitable success, and perhaps as a consequence of this, most of these countries are undergoing deep political and social changes domestically and are constructing innovative solutions to meet new international challenges. Big Power tensions continue to be played out in the neighbourhood despite the tradition of neutrality exercised by the Association of Southeast Asian Nations (ASEAN).

The **Trends in Southeast Asia** series acts as a platform for serious analyses by selected authors who are experts in their fields. It is aimed at encouraging policymakers and scholars to contemplate the diversity and dynamism of this exciting region.

THE EDITORS

Series Chairman:
    Choi Shing Kwok

Series Editor:
    Ooi Kee Beng

Editorial Committee:
    Daljit Singh
    Francis E. Hutchinson
    Norshahril Saat

The Unrealized Mahathir-Anwar Transitions: Social Divides and Political Consequences

By Khoo Boo Teik

EXECUTIVE SUMMARY

- The failure of two expected transitions of leadership from Dr Mahathir Mohamad to Anwar Ibrahim (in 1998 and 2020) are traceable beyond their personal entanglements to the social divides and political currents of their time.
- The unrealized transitions are symptomatic of a dynamic of "dysfunctional succession" that began in UMNO. Under Mahathir, the party split. Under Najib it was defeated. The condition persists in Perikatan Nasional as its head, Prime Minister Muhyiddin Yassin, has not even appointed a deputy prime minister after being in power for fifteen months.
- The unrealized transitions were a setback for a "reform agenda", which Anwar Ibrahim articulated, but which emerged from dissident movements for diverse reforms. These movements helped the multiethnic, socially inclusive, opposition to win the 14th General Election. They are only seemingly dormant because of the pandemic.
- The Pakatan Harapan regime had the best chance to supply a fresh vision, deeper social understanding, and commitment to reform. The present Perikatan Nasional regime's fixation on "Malayness" overlooks twenty years of intense intra-Malay conflicts that began with the failure of the first transition.
- As the "7th Prime Minister", Mahathir had a rare chance to redeem himself from major errors of his first twenty-two-year tenure. He squandered his chance by not honouring the Pakatan Harapan transition plan.

- Anwar Ibrahim's opponents mock him for being obsessed with wanting to be prime minister. Yet they obsessively fear his becoming prime minister. Anwar may be twice loser in political succession but "the spectre of Anwar" still haunts Malaysian political consciousness.

The Unrealized Mahathir-Anwar Transitions: Social Divides and Political Consequences

By Khoo Boo Teik[1]

> "The first three prime ministers belonged to the *bangsawan* (aristocracy). The fourth, Mahathir, began as a commoner but ended as a *bangsawan*."
>
> (A. Samad Said)[2]

> "We have an agenda. You must stick to the agenda. It is a reform agenda. We don't want just to replace the prime minister. We want to replace the damned system."
>
> (Nurul Izzah Anwar)[3]

One of the more baffling puzzles of Malaysian politics is the convoluted political relationship of Dr Mahathir Mohamad, twice Prime Minister of Malaysia (1981–2003 and 2018–20), and Anwar Ibrahim, once Deputy Prime Minister (1993–98), which thrived for many years but suddenly collapsed, and, after many more years, almost unbelievably revived, but just as incredulously crashed again.

---

[1] Khoo Boo Teik is Professor Emeritus, National Graduate Institute for Policy Studies, Tokyo; Research Fellow Emeritus, Institute of Developing Economies, Chiba, Japan; and Visiting Senior Fellow, ISEAS – Yusof Ishak Institute, Singapore (April to September 2021).

[2] Speech at a rally in Kampong Bahru, Kuala Lumpur, 8 January 2012; author's notes.

[3] Speech at the BERSIH 5 rally, Kuala Lumpur, 16 November 2016, Pantaitube "BERSIH 5 – Nurul Izzah @ KLCC", *YouTube*, 20 November 2016, at 06:00, https://www.youtube.com/watch?v=1o7QPtzYtNc (accessed 15 September 2017).

Mahathir and Anwar's political relationship formally began in March 1982. In July 1981, Mahathir became President of the United Malays National Organization (UMNO) and Prime Minister. Six months later, Anwar left Angkatan Belia Islam Malaysia (ABIM, or Malaysian Islamic Youth Movement), which he had led for eight years, to join UMNO. Thereafter, Anwar's political career blossomed. By 1993 he was UMNO Deputy President and Deputy Prime Minister. But just when he appeared to be UMNO's "anointed successor" to the prime minister, Anwar was sacked by Mahathir on 2 September 1998, expelled from UMNO the next day, arrested on 20 September, prosecuted on charges of corruption and sodomy, convicted and handed prison sentences of six years for the first charge and nine for the second. This shocking end to the Mahathir-Anwar relationship sparked a dissident movement, *Reformasi*, and inspired the opposition to battle the regime past Mahathir's retirement in November 2003.

The two men had an unexpected reconciliation in September 2016. Anwar was then in prison again although he was earlier freed in September 2004.[4] The reconciliation brought Mahathir's new party, Parti Pribumi Bersatu Malaysia (Bersatu, or United Pribumi Party of Malaysia) into the Anwar-led opposition coalition, Pakatan Harapan (Harapan, or Pact of Hope) to fight the regime of Najib Razak who was embroiled in the 1 Malaysia Development Berhad (1MDB) financial scandal.[5] There was a Harapan agreement that if Harapan won the impending general election, Mahathir would lead its government for about half of its five-year term

---

[4] The Federal Court overturned his conviction for sodomy in 2004 but the same court found him guilty of a different charge of sodomy in February 2015.

[5] For the breaking story on 1MDB, see *Sarawak Report*, "Heist of the Century: How Jho Low Used PetroSaudi as 'a Front' to Siphon Billions out of 1MDB!", *sarawakreport.org*, 28 February 2015, http://www.sarawakreport.org/2015/02/heist-of-the-century-how-jho-low-used-petrosaudi-as-a-front-to-siphon-billions-out-of-1mdb-world-exclusive/ (accessed 18 September 2017).

before handing the premiership to Anwar. At the 14th General Election (GE14) of May 2018, Harapan won and Mahathir became the "7th Prime Minister". Anwar was freed by a royal pardon and returned to Parliament after winning a by-election. In February 2020, Mahathir wrecked the planned transfer of the premiership when he moved to remain as Prime Minister without being bound to Harapan at all. His caper failed and his government collapsed. Anwar tried in vain to form a new Harapan government. But Mahathir's deputy in Bersatu, Muhyiddin Yassin, led the majority of Bersatu's Members of Parliament (MPs) to join a splinter faction from Anwar's party, Parti Keadilan Rakyat (PKR, or People's Justice Party) to form a new government in an ad hoc coalition that included the losers of GE14, namely, UMNO and Parti Islam SeMalaysia (PAS, or the Pan Malaysian Islamic Party). Consequently, the failure of the second Mahathir-Anwar transition let in a "backdoor government" that had neither an electoral mandate nor a publicly demonstrated majority in Parliament.

How did Mahathir and Anwar, two skilled politicians, become so tortuously entangled? What caused the Mahathir-Anwar leadership transition to fail twice, and to what political consequences?

Answers to such questions cannot ignore the two men's characters and traits, and ambitions and missteps. But leadership transitions are political events that take place at particular moments under specific social conditions. This essay traces the Mahathir-Anwar trajectory of concord and discord to deeper social roots and political currents. The trajectory at its height concealed dissimilarities of worldview that coincided with social divides in Malaysia. Meanwhile, contentious leadership succession in UMNO, the dominant party of the ruling coalition (Barisan Nasional, BN, or National Front), weakened the stability of the political system. By examining the two dynamics—of social transformation and strife over succession—the essay shows the deeper socio-political significance of events and details that otherwise remain personal and melodramatic with no seeming cohesiveness. Its conclusion considers the consequences of the unrealized transitions for leadership succession, a reform agenda, the condition of the political class, Mahathir's legacy, and Anwar's position.

I. ORIGINS AND DIVERGENCES: A DYNAMIC OF SOCIAL TRANSFORMATION

It is reflective, yet oddly unremarked, of Malaysia's socio-political transformation after independence that the fortunes of the nation, loosely speaking, had lain more than once in the charge of three men of Malay small-town plebeian or commoner origins. The oldest and most famous of the three is Mahathir Mohamad, the youngest child of the first headmaster of the Government English School in Alor Star, Kedah.[6] The second, also from Alor Star, and the wealthiest, is Daim Zainuddin, the youngest son of a clerk in the State Civil Service (Land Office) of Kedah.[7] Daim is best known as the Minister of Finance from 1984 to 1991 and special economic adviser to the government from time to time. The third man, something of an epic figure, is Anwar Ibrahim, the eldest son of a medical assistant in Cherok To'kun, Penang, who became an UMNO Member of Parliament (MP).[8]

I.1. Social Mobility and Plebeian Ascendancy

The three men's fathers were plebeian but not lowly.[9] On the contrary they had attained upward mobility by serving as functionaries in the colonial administration. They belonged recognizably to a respectable urban civil service salariat in an agrarian economy and largely rural society where Malay commerce was limited and Malay professionals

---

[6] Later renamed Sultan Abdul Hamid College. Alor Star, the capital of Kedah, was a small town during the youth of Mahathir and Daim.

[7] Cheong Mei Sui and Adibah Amin, *Daim: The Man Behind the Enigma* (Petaling Jaya: Pelanduk Publications, 1995), p. 7.

[8] Charles Allers, *Anwar Ibrahim: Evolution of a Muslim Democrat* (Singapore: Monsoon Books, 2014), pp. 31, 35.

[9] Mahathir's autobiography begins: "The odds had always been stacked heavily against me. I did not come from the Malay ruling elite … I … was a commoner" (Mahathir Mohamad, *A Doctor in the House: The Memoirs of Tun Dr Mahathir Mohamad* [Petaling Jaya: MPH Group Publishing, 2011], pp. 1–2). Mahathir said of his family that, "I suppose we would have been considered lower-middle class" (ibid., p. 16).

were few. From such stations and socio-spatial locations at birth, Mahathir, Daim and Anwar progressed to exalted positions in national politics and government (and big business for Daim). Whatever was exceptional about them as individuals, their shared experience of upward mobility in a single generation captured the historic ascendancy of the Malay plebeian classes, aided by the expansion of public education and urbanization after independence, and especially under the New Economic Policy (NEP). The rise of Mahathir, Daim and Anwar captured the enormity of that social ascendancy when they occupied the pinnacle of national financial and economic stewardship beginning with Daim's appointment as the Minister of Finance in 1984. Previous ministers of finance had come first from upper-class families of Chinese commercial prominence and then of Malay nobility, even royalty.

In politics and government, the three men shared many views on economic development—a compelling BN and UMNO priority. Despite their similar social origins, their own personalities, ideas and aspirations were variously shaped by individual experiences and influences. Mahathir's worldview was formed by pre- and post-war Malay nationalism. Anwar was much influenced by student activism and Islamic thought in the decade after independence. Daim was drawn to business during the first NEP decade. As state interventionism, changing capitalism, and extensive social policy transformed the economy and society, these men found different meanings in social mobility and the goals of economic advancement. Their worldviews, social affinities and political aspirations showed subtle divergences.

I.2. Divergent Paths

Mahathir has been a doctor, writer, businessman and politician.[10] His career path was clear in its direction and aims. He became what he most wanted to be, a national leader who had the power to implement his

---

[10] This profile of Mahathir is drawn from Khoo Boo Teik, *Paradoxes of Mahathirism: An Intellectual Biography of Mahathir Mohamad* (Kuala Lumpur: Oxford University Press, 1995), and *Beyond Mahathir: Malaysian Politics and Its Discontents* (London and New York: Zed Books, 2003).

5

own ideas on developing the country. In his imaginary, things began and ended with the economy, be it national, regional or global, and one's place in it. Mahathir measured success and failure—whether personal, communal, national, regional or international—by the yardsticks of absolute and comparative economic performance and wealth. He spoke in pressing terms of changing the values of Malays to extricate them from their condition of "relative backwardness" and in crude tones of having as many Malay millionaires as non-Malay ones. He spoke ambitiously of freeing the country from its underdeveloped status or resentfully of watching national development being subverted by immoral foreign currency speculators. He had a multidimensional preoccupation with worldly pursuits tied to the production, acquisition, distribution and preservation of wealth by all the social groups with whom he was bonded. Above all, he thrilled to the grandeur of his modernizing nationalist-capitalist project, his life's work.

Daim also had a clear path from the professions to business. In outlook he belonged with Mahathir's developmental project but notably from another angle. Daim personified the ambitions, and achievements up to a point, of an emerging NEP-justified and state-spawned class of big Malay capitalists. In business, a combination of promising projects, lucrative contracts, risk taking, and diligence allowed him to speed past intermediate stops to high corporate success.[11] Daim embodied "the spirit of Malay capitalism". "You must enjoy business," he said, "enjoy making money and enjoy thinking of ways to make more money with the money you have."[12] He claimed that he could be a tough Minister of Finance because of his lack of political partisanship and ambition. "I am a politician through and through," he explained, "I was just reluctant to hold office."[13] In fact, he had long been involved in politics, including an early "covert role" helping the Federal government to manipulate the fall of the Stephen Kalong Ningkan government in Sarawak.[14] Daim

---

[11] See Cheong and Adibah, *Daim*, pp. 52–60, for some of Daim's corporate deals, with explanations of controversial points.

[12] Ibid., p. 16.

[13] Ibid., p. 35.

[14] Ibid., pp. 22–23.

regarded himself as a model for aspiring Malay capitalists who should operate by a mode idealized by Mahathir: take opportunities from the state but work "damn hard" to prosper.[15]

Mahathir and Daim took the trend of upward mobility to its social and political conclusion: the one gained state power by being the first commoner to be prime minister, and the other corporate influence being once the Minister of Finance, the UMNO Treasurer, and a prominent capitalist at the same time. Together they personified Malaysia Incorporated,[16] the name Mahathir gave to his state-capital alliance, and shaped the commercial world of the new rich, in particular, the new Malay rich. Mahathir and Daim epitomized a social order led by a fusion of Melayu Baru (New Malay) and Bangsa Malaysia (Malaysian nationality).[17]

Anwar was the odd man out. His trek from plebeian origins to political eminence veered from Mahathir's and Daim's pathways. Anwar was a student activist, a civil society leader, a political prisoner, a dissident Islamist, and an ally of the opposition before he joined UMNO. In his youthful Islamic radicalism, he was scathing towards post-independent "neocolonial development" that could not end poverty and inequality but reproduced social vices and moral hollowness. He wanted holistic development that valued rounded education, moral renewal, personal modesty, and social welfare. He was putatively anti-Mahathirist, being less bound to ethnicity, nationalism, materialism, and authoritarian leanings.[18] Anwar once recalled that in his Budget Speeches, "I made

---

[15] Daim said, "How did I succeed? I worked damn hard, and when I was not working, I was thinking ... The Malays have to learn to work and sweat for their money" (ibid., pp. 18–19). A different view of Daim's "business methods" is given by Barry Wain, *Malaysian Maverick: Mahathir Mohamad in Turbulent Times* (Basingstoke: Palgrave Macmillan, 2009), pp. 133–34.

[16] Khoo, *Paradoxes of Mahathirism*, pp. 132–34.

[17] Ibid., pp. 327–38.

[18] He was opposed to detention without trial under the Internal Security Act (ISA): "I refused to sign ISA orders while being Acting PM. I'd never sign. I told them, 'Wait for PM'" (Anwar Ibrahim, Talk in George Town, Penang, 4 June 2006; author's notes).

some reference to Vision 2020 merely to survive."[19] His 1996 book, *The Asian Renaissance*, criticized state economic intervention where it was not checked by transparency, accountability and social justice. Islamic principles permitted market-based accumulation of wealth but Anwar was not lured by the enriching upward mobility of the new rich like Daim. Minister of Finance Anwar patronized big business, and was not above using it for political purposes but he did not trust a strong state *and* an untrammelled market *and* aggrandizing corporations. He leaned ideologically towards a vague "moral economy" that was sensitive to the quotidian pressures, household insecurities, and modest expectations of social mobility common to plebeian life in semi-rural areas, small towns and even big cities.[20] An ascendant Anwar had to acculturate himself to state and big business. Yet he envisioned a caring civil society (*masyarakat madani*)[21] for the plebeian masses who fell short of Mahathir's super-nationalist mission or Daim's super-capitalist ambition.

II. POLITICAL SUCCESSION: A DYNAMIC OF STRIFE[22]

The political milieu of the Mahathir-Anwar transition was framed by a dynamic of leadership succession which operated at UMNO's apex and ultimately decided who would be prime minister and deputy prime minister. From the collapse of the Alliance government after 13 May 1969 to Anwar's repeat election as UMNO Deputy President in 1996, succession in UMNO was marked by an inconstant balance of power

---

[19] Anwar Ibrahim, "I am Committed and Determined", *Aliran Monthly* 27, no. 1 (2007), p. 5.

[20] That it blended with plebeian concerns over tolls, inflation and crime in the cities widened Anwar's support base when he led a revived opposition coalition.

[21] See Khoo Boo Teik, *The Making of Anwar Ibrahim's "Humane Economy"*, Trends in Southeast Asia, no. 18/2020 (Singapore: ISEAS – Yusof Ishak Institute, 2020).

[22] This section is adapted from Khoo Boo Teik, "Democracy and Transition in Malaysia: An Analysis of the Problems of Political Succession", *Macalester International*, Vol. 12, Article 11 (Fall 2002): 59–79.

between its top leadership and the "party at large". The result was alternation between stable and volatile succession.

II.1. Preserving Prerogative in Crises

The first instance of succession arose at a moment of national emergency. Prime Minister Tunku Abdul Rahman was edged out of power after "May 13". Deputy Prime Minister Tun Abdul Razak headed a National Operations Council (NOC) that ruled while Parliament was suspended. Sixteen months later, the Tunku retired and was officially replaced by Razak. Thus, the first transition in premiership happened with "no immediate break in leadership and no succession crisis".[23]

Razak picked Dr Ismail Abdul Rahman, for his deputy but Ismail died in August 1973. Razak then selected Hussein Onn. But Razak died in January 1976. Before Hussein could decide, UMNO's three vice-presidents, Ghafar Baba, Tengku Razaleigh Hamzah and Mahathir, jointly informed him that he had to choose one of them for his deputy premier.[24] Hussein chose Mahathir, who was third among equals, so to speak, having secured third place in the 1975 contests for the vice-presidents. Ghafar, who had received first place, withdrew from the Cabinet in protest. Razaleigh bided his time. From Razak to Hussein, no one questioned the prerogative of the prime minister to appoint his deputy.

II.2. Party Mandate and Implosive Factionalism

In 1981, Hussein decided to retire after the June UMNO general assembly. Hussein endorsed Mahathir as his successor, which no one disputed. Just as Hussein bypassed seniority by picking Mahathir for his deputy, so Mahathir bypassed seniority by leaving it to the party to

---

[23] Gordon Means, *Malaysian Politics: The Second Generation* (Singapore: Oxford University Press, 1991), p. 19.

[24] We now have the word of Tommy Thomas (*My Story: Justice in the Wilderness* [Petaling Jaya: SIRD, 2021], pp. 86–87) that Hussein originally favoured Ghazali Shafie who was not one of the three vice-presidents.

elect his deputy.[25] The decision favoured Musa Hitam,[26] who won the contest for deputy president against Razaleigh. By one view, Mahathir, who would only be president after the UMNO general assembly, "had no choice but to concede to the party delegates to decide their choice for Deputy President".[27] A different view held that that "concession" was a ploy to deny Razaleigh whom Mahathir considered a more dangerous rival than Musa.[28] The 1981 Razaleigh-Musa battle set a precedent: an aspiring successor required an electoral mandate. The party at large would not passively endorse its president's choice of deputy. But now UMNO could not immunize succession against factionalism as shown by the repeat Musa-Razaleigh contest of 1984 (also won by Musa).

In February 1986, amidst many crises, Musa resigned as Deputy Prime Minister but remained UMNO Deputy President. Razaleigh was again bypassed when Mahathir picked Ghafar Baba for his deputy. From there, an open battle for UMNO's top posts spun out of control in 1987. The party was split into "Team A", led by Mahathir and Ghafar, and "Team B", led by Razaleigh and Musa. Razaleigh challenged Mahathir for the presidency while Ghafar took on Musa. Mahathir defeated Razaleigh by forty-three votes, and Ghafar beat Musa by forty.[29] All Team B ministers and deputy ministers resigned or were purged from the Cabinet. This fiercest of all UMNO elections spilt beyond the

---

[25] This was only UMNO's second contest for the deputy presidency. The first was an uneventful affair Razak won against Ismail in 1956.

[26] A plebeian, too, Musa was the son of a Central Electricity Board meter reader in Johore Bahru, Johor (Bruce Gale, *Musa Hitam: A Political Biography* [Petaling Jaya: Eastern Universities Press, 1982], p. 3).

[27] Mahathir "was generally known to be allied to Datuk Musa before" (A. Ghani Ismail, *Razaleigh Lawan Musa: Pusingan Kedua 1984* [Razaleigh Battles Musa: Second Round 1984] [Taiping, Perak: IJS Communications, 1983], p. 16).

[28] "Apparently Tengku Razaleigh truly believed that he had a 'pact' whereby he would be appointed to the posts of UMNO Deputy President and Deputy Prime Minister when Datuk Hussein Onn retired in the same manner that Datuk Hussein and Datuk Seri Mahathir were respectively appointed to the number two post" (ibid., p. 11).

[29] The Ghafar-Musa contest was marred by 41 "spoilt" votes. Those were almost certainly cast by Razaleigh supporters who refused to vote for Musa after his victories over Razaleigh in 1981 and 1984.

party into the courts—which de-registered UMNO as a party because of breaches of its electoral rules—and the bureaucracy which allowed Mahathir to establish a "New UMNO" that excluded Razaleigh and other Team B stalwarts. The latter formed an opposition party, Parti Semangat 46 (S46, or Spirit of 46 Party), that fought UMNO unsuccessfully in the 1990 and 1995 general elections. The aftermath of UMNO's 1987 succession struggle need not be discussed further.

II.3. Curbing Elections

The next UMNO succession episode arose in 1993. Learning from 1987, UMNO's leadership amended the party's rules on its triennial elections. The new rules had conservative intent: to centralize authority, consolidate incumbency, pre-empt any disruptive challenge, and protect the continuity of leadership. The president became too powerful to be challenged. Anwar, however, decided to fight Ghafar for deputy president. Mahathir's empathy seemed to be divided between his old loyalist (Ghafar) and his ambitious protégé (Anwar). When Anwar triumphed, Mahathir made him Deputy Prime Minister, effectively accepting the party's mandate. To forestall any challenge to himself in the subsequent UMNO election of 1996, Mahathir added rules that kept the party's top two leaders unopposed. So, Anwar was reaffirmed Deputy President, and regarded as the "anointed successor".

III. THE FIRST FAILED TRANSITION

Many commentators attributed Malaysia's pre-crisis economic growth in the 1990s to "Anwar's pro-market reforms".[30] They might more

---

[30] John Dori, *Standing Up for Democracy and Economic Reform in Malaysia*, The Heritage Foundation, 16 November 1998, https://www.heritage.org/asia/report/standing-democracy-and-economic-reform-malaysia (accessed 5 July 2021). For recent and typical praise of Anwar for "promoting market reforms that spurred Malaysia's rapid economic growth in the 1990s", see Carl Gershman, "Introduction of Anwar Ibrahim", *Fifteenth Annual Seymour Martin Lipset Lecture on Democracy in the World*, National Endowment for Democracy, 11 February 2019, https://www.ned.org/introduction-of-anwar-ibrahim/ (accessed 15 May 2019).

fairly have credited Mahathir and Daim—as Anwar did[31]—with their "pro-business" measures for reviving the economy from the recession of the mid-1980s. Mahathir and Daim privatized (state-owned assets and large-scale projects), liberalized (the investment regime), and deregulated (the capital market most of all). They launched an austerity drive of fiscal discipline, budget cuts, a freeze on civil service recruitment, reductions in subsidies, curtailment of funds for state-owned enterprises (SOEs) and off-budget agencies, higher interest rates, and lower liquidity in the financial system.[32] All that was "bitter medicine", which Daim imposed administratively and Mahathir defended politically.[33] They rode out the grievances of UMNO's traditional bases of support—the party ranks, the civil service, the lower-level Malay business class, and the Malay community generally. The Mahathir regime even suspended the NEP in September 1986. Stripped of officialese, the austerity measures could be likened to homegrown "International Monetary Fund (IMF) structural adjustment without the IMF".[34]

III.1. Formula of Success, Recipe for Disaster

A grassroots politician, Mahathir loyalist and Cabinet member, Anwar witnessed the economic tensions and political reactions that included

---

[31] In his first Budget Speech, Anwar praised Daim: his "decisive and brave steps strengthened the national economic situation" and his punctilious servicing of external debt "not only relieved the country of a huge debt burden but started a practice of early debt repayment". See Supply Bill 1992, *Parliamentary Debates*, House of Representatives, Eighth Parliament, First Session, 1 November 1991, column 12702.

[32] For an unsurpassed analysis of the policies and politics of this conjuncture, see Khoo Khay Jin, "The Grand Vision: Mahathir and Modernisation", in *Fragmented Vision: Culture and Politics in Contemporary Malaysia*, edited by Joel S Kahn and Francis Loh Kok Wah (Sydney: Allen & Unwin, 1992), pp. 44–76.

[33] The "medicine has been indeed bitter for virtually everyone except for a fortunate few", it was said of the austerity drive (ibid. p. 54).

[34] To recall the charge, with its insinuation of betrayal, made against Anwar after his fall. "At home", Mahathir wrote long after the crisis, "Anwar started what became known as the 'IMF solution without the IMF'" (*Doctor in the House*, p. 672).

the UMNO split of 1987–88. As Minister of Finance, Anwar normalized the regime's narrative that the pains of the 1980s were the gains of the 1990s, and that the robustness of the economy proved the efficacy of the Mahathir-Daim formula for crisis management. Perhaps Anwar could apply the formula if another crisis erupted.

The 1997 financial crisis brought an externally induced, speculation-driven depreciation of the national currency that destabilized the financial system and wrought economic disaster. Against such disorder, the market could give no relief in the old forms of foreign direct investment and private sector investment. Indeed, a finicky global market of high finance was itself the bane. It was one of Anwar's tasks to calm a volatile market with "confidence-boosting" measures that accorded with the technocratic options of Bank Negara, the orthodoxy of the international financial institutions, and the demands of the global financial market. Those measures had Cabinet approval, Anwar insisted, but their impact approached the severity of the conditionalities of lending that the IMF imposed on Indonesia, Thailand, and South Korea.[35]

Anwar had evidently not prepared for an alien scenario in which a "correct" formula applied to subordinate classes would be the "wrong" one to use against a set of rich and powerful interests. The 1997 financial crisis threatened the politico-corporate oligarchy, especially its precarious Malay segment, with imminent collapse. At once Mahathir sensed the danger even if he took longer to grasp the systemic underpinnings of the crisis.[36] He denounced currency speculation and wanted to change the rules of the domestic share market. His reactions drove share prices and

---

[35] The country "was going into an abyss", says Francis Yeoh, head of the powerful YTL Corp. infrastructure company and a long-time acquaintance of both men. "Much more of that, and we would have shut our doors" (Ian Johnson, "Intimate Enemies: How Malaysia's Rulers Devoured Each Other and Much They Built", *Wall Street Journal*, 30 October 1998).

[36] Ironically, Mahathir learned the complexities of the currency trade from Nor Mohamed Yakcop, under whose currency trading Bank Negara lost a huge amount of money in 1992 (Wain, *Malaysian Maverick*, pp. 166–72). See Mahathir, *Doctor in the House*, pp. 673–78.

the value of the ringgit further down.[37] Yet his "irrationality" revealed sharp instincts of state and class: Mahathir feared the diminution of state power and the demise of domestic corporations. In the 1980s, the austerity imposed by him and Daim "naturally won the approval" of IMF.[38] But now IMF-style austerity would be sheer toxin:

> IMF wants us … to increase the interest rates, to reduce credit, to increase taxes. Now all three of these things would bankrupt our companies. When you reduce the currency by 50 per cent and the share prices by more than 50 per cent, then all of the companies find they cannot pay their debts, because they borrowed using their shares as collateral, on the basis of 80 per cent of the value of the shares. Now the fall in shares has made the borrowing much bigger and they have to top up. Now how do you top up in a situation when the economy is not doing well?[39]

Debates over policy responses to the crisis were typically conducted with the economistic jargon of dampening market volatility, monetary injections, pump priming, or "quantitative easing".[40] Mahathir's new course of treatment simply opposed IMF rationality: not austerity but rescue, not credit crunch but looser liquidity, not higher but lower interest rates, not a stricter but more lenient definition of a non-performing loan, not forced corporate insolvency but negotiated debt rescheduling, and, above all, not the "fire sale" of prime assets to foreigners but their nationalization with public funds. Mahathir's approach staked out nothing less than a battle for class survival, for saving the social world of the corporate elites from collapsing.

---

[37] See Jomo K.S., "From Currency Crisis to Recession", in *Malaysian Eclipse: Economic Crisis and Recovery*, edited by Jomo K.S. (London and New York: Zed Books, 2001), pp. 1–46, and Wain, *Malaysian Maverick*, pp. 106–7.

[38] Although the initial push for austerity "apparently came from the technocrats in Bank Negara" (Khoo, "The Grand Vision", p. 54).

[39] Mahathir, quoted in "How Dare You Say These Things!", *Time*, 15 June 1998.

[40] A euphemism the US made famous in the global crisis ten years later.

III.2. The Vengeance of Class

To bail out the wealthy and powerful using public funds risked a popular backlash: would it not smack of "collusion, corruption and cronyism"?[41] But what was the Minister of Finance for, if not to hold the fort of state and oligarchy not just against the global market—the regime's rationale—but against a distressed *rakyat*?[42]

Neither Anwar nor Mahathir was completely correct or wholly wrong in handling the crisis at various points between 2 July 1997 and 1 September 1998.[43] They could not avoid making policy reversals and tactical turns.[44] On one matter, Anwar baulked.[45] Mahathir blamed the crisis entirely on external sources,[46] thereby absolving domestic corporations of culpability in their misfortune. Anwar vacillated: what should be done about those corporations and their owners who included Mahathir's children and tycoons close to him? They, who had grown "rich beyond the dreams of avarice", scampered to be saved. Anwar had preached frugality, fiscal prudence and the sound management of one's finances as good governance, moral values, and even religious injunctions. His Budget Speeches had warned against the frenzied accumulation and excessive consumption of wealth, and urged wise preparation during "years of plenty" for "years of drought".[47] Maybe Anwar hesitated to

---

[41] To use the slogan of *Reformasi* in Indonesia during the same crisis.

[42] "The people", a catch-all category into which Anwar could toss the hoi polloi, the masses, the grassroots, the subaltern classes, the disenfranchised, and whoever else had been passed over by frenetic economic growth and restless material prosperity.

[43] After Anwar's fall, highly partisan views conveniently drew stark and irreconcilable differences between Anwar and Mahathir (and Daim) (Jomo K.S., "Acknowledgements", in *Malaysian Eclipse: Economic Crisis and Recovery*, p. xxi).

[44] Ibid., fn. 2, pp. xix–xxi, and fn. 3, p. xxi.

[45] "Beginning from the UEM-Renong episode from November 1997, Anwar probably resisted Mahathir-Daim pressures to bail out some politically well-connected business interests" (ibid., p. xx).

[46] It was equally false to blame the crisis solely on domestic flaws (ibid., p. xv).

[47] Khoo, *The Making of Anwar's "Humane Economy"*, pp. 11–12.

rescue the elites if he had to sacrifice the social classes below them.[48] He had, romantically, imagined the crisis to lead to "a leaner and revitalized market economy, based on fairness and competition on a level playing field, where big corporations, *small businesses and all citizens have equal access to capital and resources*".[49] Whatever were his political calculations,[50] the vestiges of class came into their own. Unlike Mahathir and Daim, Anwar had not travelled a pathway of upward mobility that bound him to those who occupied the apex of state and class power.[51] His "soul" was plebeian after all.[52] By the time Anwar wrote of "creative destruction", "cleansing", "level playing field", and discarding "old modes of thinking",[53] however, the technocratic correctness of his policies no longer mattered. Many among the beleaguered elites took his criticism of "collusion, corruption and nepotism" as a foreboding of what he could do to their social world should he assume prime ministerial powers. To many of the elites, the "anointed successor" was no more than a plebeian pretender, and had to go.

III.3. The Retribution of Politics

For about sixteen years, Anwar led a charmed life in UMNO. He rose in the party as if unstoppably. He had his detractors, of course, who resented him as an impatient interloper with anti-UMNO antecedents. But he

---

[48] The direct threat to the subaltern classes was not the collapse of conglomerates they did not own or the loss of vast fortunes they did not possess. If the economy collapsed, they would suffer higher unemployment, inflation, depreciation of what assets they had, and opportunities for their children.

[49] Anwar Ibrahim, "A Wave of Creative Destruction Is Sweeping Asia", *New York Times*, 2 June 1998; emphasis added.

[50] It would be naïve to discount his ambition.

[51] He tried horse-riding but stopped after injuring himself from a fall. How more illustrative can it get of his failure to be "one of them"?

[52] How could he not be so? His musical tastes ran to local Malay pop songs and tunes from Hindustani films.

[53] He had stopped being anti-Western, he was not enamoured of the state, and the collapse of the USSR might have taken him closer to being pro-market; see Anwar Ibrahim, *The Asian Renaissance* (Singapore: Marshall Cavendish, 1996).

had supporters who glimpsed UMNO's future in him.[54] In 1993, Anwar considered it politically strategic, even if others thought it culturally incorrect, for him to challenge Ghafar as soon as UMNO had recovered from its post-1987 chaos. If he aspired to be prime minister, Anwar had to be just a step away from the UMNO President's post, not least because the president had had heart operations in 1989.[55]

Its history of strife over succession hung like a nightmare over UMNO. Anwar had to worry that he would fall short of his goal if he waited too long for his turn to be prime minister. Mahathir would not countenance another Razaleigh-style challenge against him. Mahathir, who knew UMNO's shifting alliances and power balances, was liable to see a demurring deputy as a threat. Around 1987, economic recession and the Mahathir-Daim austerity had fuelled so much discontent that it only took Razaleigh's willingness to "take up the cudgels" for the party's malcontents to carry Team B very close to ousting Mahathir.[56] If the financial crisis deteriorated, who could rule out party disaffection coalescing around Anwar? Speculation was rife in 1997–98 that Anwar had extended his influence over UMNO.

Mahathir would not test the accuracy of the speculation. He could be sentimental over UMNO's origins but the party was no sacred cow for him. He had demonstrated before that only state power was effective in emergencies.[57] He opted to use the state to crush the *idea* of a party rebellion long before anyone had a chance to organize it. The destruction of Anwar's career by his dismissal, humiliation, prosecution and imprisonment was as much a move to contain discontent in UMNO. That

---

[54] See Ghani Ismail, *Razaleigh Lawan Musa*, pp. 61, 64–65.

[55] Mahathir, *Doctor in the House*, pp. 572–76. No UMNO leader would forget that Ismail and Razak had died in office from illness, while Hussein retired due to poor health. Mahathir thought he might need another operation ten years later, that is, 1999 (ibid., p. 579).

[56] Khoo, "The Grand Vision", p. 48.

[57] His resort to police repression in October 1987, application of bureaucratic authority to register "New UMNO" in 1988, and judicial influence to impeach the Lord Chief Justice and other Supreme Court judges in 1998—all linked to the 1987 UMNO split—had proven that.

tactic of "killing the chicken to frighten the monkey" worked: barring a few ineffectual voices and Anwar loyalists, the UMNO elite did not bestir itself to defend the party's "anointed successor".

It is hazardous to be Minister of Finance during a recession,[58] and it is risky to be Deputy Prime Minister when one disagrees with the Prime Minister's major policies.[59] Anwar discovered that it was worse to hold both positions concurrently when he diverged from Mahathir's scheme of crisis management while the economic debacle threw up the question of political succession. In a word, Anwar's first political defeat came at the convergence of the two dynamics of social transformation and political succession.

IV. THE SECOND FAILED TRANSITION

The beginning of this essay gives the background to the second Mahathir-Anwar transition, planned but unrealized. Although the plan was tied to the politics of the twenty years from Anwar's fall to the BN's defeat at GE14, its origin lay at a peculiar juncture between February 2015 and September 2016. There is not much replication here of "blow-by-blow" accounts, available elsewhere, of the manoeuvres made by different antagonists that unravelled the transition. Instead, a "big picture" is developed of another convergence of social divide and succession strife which made it such that to thwart the transition was to subvert the Harapan government.

IV.1. Rise Against the Regime

The definitive feature of the politics of 1998–2018 was what the opposition called *Kebangkitan Rakyat*, or "The Rising of the People".[60]

---

[58] See Cheong and Adibah, *Daim*, pp. 49 and 72, on Daim's issues with "popularity".

[59] As Musa found out (Khoo, *Paradoxes of Mahathirism*, p. 229).

[60] There are many *Himpunan Kebangkitan Rakyat* video clips. For example, see "HKR KL 112 Ucapan Dato' Seri Anwar Ibrahim", SelangorTV, *YouTube*, 12 January 2013, https://www.youtube.com/watch?v=hlrugUJ-GFQ

The term referred to a popular non-violent uprising that opposed the regime headed by Mahathir, then by his successor, Abdullah Ahmad Badawi, and, lastly, by Abdullah's replacement, Najib Razak.

The singular character of this uprising was the inventive ability of the broad opposition front to expand the social sources of dissent by adding non-Malay constituencies to the original Malay base, and building alliances with movements such as BERSIH and HINDRAF.[61] By mobilizing on the ground, even across the world, and creating "imagined cyber communities of dissent", dissident activists blended separate voter segments into an insurgent electorate.[62] What began as inchoate Malay cultural revulsion against Anwar's *aib* (shame) grew into a dissident movement, *Reformasi*, that impelled the opposition parties to form alternative coalitions to fight the BN for power.

The animus of *Kebangkitan Rakyat* was the plebeian reformism of the insurgent electorate. Widening dissent made the scope of reform more inclusive of social demands while the opposition parties muted their ideological differences to build a united front. A "reform agenda" was culled from party platforms before the opposition coalition issued common electoral manifestos for the 13th General Election (GE13, 2013) and GE14. The plebeian reformism found a coherent articulation in Anwar's conception of a "humane economy", the gist of PKR's *Malaysian Economic Agenda* and *A New Dawn for Malaysia*.[63]

The historic achievements of successive alternative coalitions were: the losses inflicted on UMNO in the 10th General Election (GE10, 1999); a parliamentary breakthrough in the 12th General Election (GE12, 2008); the gain of a majority popular vote at GE13; and victory over BN in GE14.

---

[61] BERSIH is the Malay acronym for the Coalition for Clean and Fair Elections, HINDRAF the acronym for the Hindu Rights Action Front.

[62] It required imagination and a sense of common purpose for members and supporters of different opposition parties to vote for parties they previously did not support.

[63] Khoo, *The Making of Anwar's "Humane Economy"*, pp. 13–20.

IV.2. Towards Reconciliation

Before 2015, Mahathir was dismayed by the opposition's growing threat to UMNO. He blamed the regime's weaknesses on the poor leadership of Abdullah Badawi and Najib Razak. Yet, things had gone awry as soon as Anwar fell.

Every gain that Mahathir sought by dismissing Anwar was upended. Mahathir cowed UMNO only to see its core constituency, the Malay masses, reject UMNO as never before.[64] He immunized his corporate rescue plan from dissent within the government only to face popular condemnation of the corruption of his "opulent and greedy clique".[65] He and UMNO expected Anwar to suffer the "Harun Idris syndrome" of fading politically in jail;[66] instead, an energized opposition adopted a reinvented Anwar as its leader. Mahathir used state power to suppress Anwar's party influence but Anwar mobilized civil society dissent against the state. And although Mahathir meant to finish off Anwar's career, UMNO's losses in GE10 hastened Mahathir's departure from office.[67]

That should have been the end of active politics for Mahathir. But in 2015 three developments jolted the political terrain. In February, Anwar was again jailed while PAS Spiritual Leader Nik Abdul Aziz Nik Mat died. Anwar's leadership had held the Pakatan Rakyat together. Nik Aziz had implacably opposed any PAS cooperation with UMNO. With Anwar and Nik Aziz absent, no one could stop PAS from leaving Pakatan and tilting towards UMNO. Then it was the regime's turn to be battered by domestic and international judicial investigations of Najib's complicity

---

[64] Philip Khoo, "Thinking the Unthinkable: A Malaysia Not Governed by the BN?", *Aliran Monthly* 19, no. 5 (1999): 2–8.

[65] Anwar blamed such a clique for his downfall (Permatang Pauh Declaration, Penang, 12 September 1998).

[66] On the Harun case, see Harold Crouch, *Government and Society in Malaysia* (Sydney: Allen & Unwin, 1996), pp. 100–4.

[67] Maznah Mohamad, "The Contest for Malay Votes in 1999: UMNO's Most Historic Challenge", in *New Politics in Malaysia*, edited by Francis Loh and Johan Saravanamuttu (Singapore: Institute of Southeast Asian Studies, 2003), pp. 66–86, gives an analysis of UMNO's loss of the Malay popular vote in 1999.

in the "1MDB scandal". Taking a leaf out of Mahathir's book, Najib dismissed his Deputy Prime Minister for questioning his conduct.[68]

An unstable juncture gave Mahathir a fresh opening. As all political combatants reappraised their strength, Mahathir abandoned Najib and UMNO. Mahathir was actually isolated. Over the 1MDB issue, he could not get Najib to repent, let alone resign; he could not move UMNO to discard its tainted leader; and he could not persuade the Malay Rulers to dismiss a discredited prime minister. So, while calling on citizens to save Malaysia from kleptocracy, Mahathir approached the opposition to make common cause against Najib and UMNO. At first Anwar rejected Mahathir's overture out of hand, but relented at the urging of his coalition and civil society allies. An Anwar-Mahathir rapprochement was achieved. It was a tactical exercise in mutual opportunism but with it the opposition had gone "to hell and back".[69]

IV.3. Behind Reconciliation

Why should Mahathir be so desperate to fight Najib, whom he preferred to Abdullah for prime minister, and UMNO which Mahathir had backed all the while? In public, Mahathir declared it his patriotic duty to stop Najib from destroying the country. That sounded like a plausible motive when a ninety-two-year-old patriarch explained it to those who were too young to relive the contempt for *Mahafiraun*,[70] too old to disparage a seeming act of contrition,[71] or too fired by years of dissident campaign to miss a historic chance to defeat UMNO.

---

[68] Also purged were Shafie Apdal, UMNO vice-president and a senior minister, and, later, Mahathir's son, Mukhriz Mahathir, Menteri Besar (Chief Minister) of Kedah.

[69] As wryly noted by a DAP strategist (Liew Chin Tong, "The 100-day Countdown to a New Malaysia", *Malaysiakini*, 28 January 2018, https://www.malaysiakini.com/news/410277 [accessed 28 January 2018].)

[70] "Great Pharaoh", the label which *Reformasi* dissidents used to denounce Mahathir for his tyranny.

[71] Mahathir once apologized to Anwar's family for their suffering but he never admitted any mistake in his maltreatment of Anwar.

There is another way to interpret Mahathir's move by recalling the dynamic of social transformation that presaged the first failed transition. He sensed two dangers to the elite, corporate, and oligarchic interests of which he was the patron.

The first danger came from "below", that is, Anwar and the opposition. By GE13, the opposition had grown to monstrous proportions and stalemated BN in Peninsular Malaysia, the principal political terrain. No UMNO veteran could assume that BN would hold off an opposition whose strength drew from popular demands for reform. If the BN fell, the corporate and monopoly interests of the oligarchy, elite, new rich, or "opulent clique" could be exposed to Anwar's reform agenda.

The second danger came from "above", "Najib's kleptocracy". Its plunder so endangered the economy and financial system as to threaten the general fortune of the oligarchy. Besides, as more 1MDB revelations emerged, the response from "above" was to expel the few UMNO leaders who criticized Najib.

Facing external defeat and unpredictable change, or internal rot and implosion, Mahathir sought an alliance "below".[72] He left UMNO with a small fraction of the party leadership. They were joined by some of the Old Guard of the Mahathir era—Daim, Sanusi Junid, Rafidah Aziz and others. This elite segment looked to a "new" politics rather than be crushed between populist reformism and immovable kleptocracy. If the opposition won GE14—improbable but not impossible—they hoped to limit and guide the reform agenda. If Mahathir insinuated himself into the leadership of a new coalition, he could neutralize the threats from above and below. The Mahathir-Anwar transition was fine in principle. As for handing power to Anwar, Mahathir would cross that bridge when he came to it.

---

[72] "For [Mahathir] the Pakatan Harapan represented the only way … to remove the kleptocrats within UMNO. He felt that UMNO could not be reformed from within as those in power were too entrenched, so he needed to join up with DAP and PKR to cleanse UMNO of the 'crooks'" (Jeyakumar Devaraj, "The Meltdown of Pakatan Harapan", Parti Sosialis Malaysia, 2 March 2020).

IV.4. Making History

The circumstances of 2015–16 befuddled all prospective contestants in GE14. The opposition had a coalition but no leader.[73] The man who offered himself as a stand-in leader had no party, never mind a coalition. The regime had state power and an old base but its prime minister no longer had legitimacy. And dissident civil society had gained a high degree of legitimacy but had no other alternative. In that political flux, alliances of convenience were formed—openly between Harapan and Shafie Apdal's Parti Warisan Sabah (Warisan, or Sabah Heritage Party), or coquettishly between UMNO and PAS. The Anwar-Mahathir reconciliation symbolized a plebeian-oligarchic alignment that created synergies in mass mobilization and produced catharses that allayed public fears of destabilization that might arise from "regime change".[74] The opposition's gamble paid off. At GE14, the UMNO regime was defeated for the first time ever in sixty-one years. "Regime change", which almost all observers said was impossible, had been achieved bloodlessly by an insurgent electorate. The latter's spirited mobilization overwhelmed the structures of power and domination.

In bringing Harapan to power, and making Mahathir the "7th Prime Minister", the electorate reared the head of another Mahathir-Anwar transition. The post-GE14 milieu brought back the social divide and succession strife, albeit in altered ways, that had previously unravelled Mahathir-Anwar transition. This time the social dynamic pitted Mahathir and his oligarchic segment against the reform agenda of the plebeian classes. The second dynamic added other "PM wannabes" against Anwar.

---

[73] If Anwar were not in jail, Mahathir would not have joined the opposition to play second fiddle to Anwar.

[74] Harapan hoped that Mahathir as prime minister-designate would overcome the reluctance of many Malay voters to vote against UMNO out of their long distrust of the "Chinese DAP".

IV.5. The Unbearable Burden of Reform

After he met Mahathir on 5 September 2016, Anwar told journalists that Mahathir had pledged his support for the reform agenda.[75] Did Anwar believe that? Or was he being diplomatic to mollify his family, party members, coalition allies, and other supporters who were unforgiving of Mahathir? What was the "reform agenda" to which Anwar referred? Did Mahathir accept it?

Four major points in the *Malaysian Economic Agenda*,[76] issued in 2007 for GE12, are sufficient to outline Anwar's agenda. First, he wanted to end the government's "anti-market policies designed to benefit itself and its cronies, at the expense of ordinary Malaysians".[77] He would replace the prevailing, "heavily-regulated market, coupled with highly opaque government operations" with a "well-regulated market, with a government willing to enforce contracts and deal fairly with the people".[78] Second, he opposed existing privatization as the "negative legacy of Mahathirism"[79]—of "privatizing profits and nationalizing losses"— that resulted in national fiscal deficit for over a decade and a half.[80] He wanted to tackle "the award of contracts, concessions and procurements by secret tender, direct negotiations … not in accordance with correct procedures and formalities",[81] by which corruption "penetrated all parts of government, the private sector and political parties especially UMNO".[82] Third, Anwar vowed to "dismantle networks of corruption, monopolies

---

[75] "Anwar: Mahathir Supports Reform Agenda", KiniTV, *YouTube*, 5 September 2016, https://www.youtube.com/watch?v=H4ygrDXfW40 (accessed 5 September 2016).

[76] Hereafter cited as MEA in the footnotes.

[77] Parti Keadilan Rakyat (PKR), *A New Dawn for Malaysia*, 2008: Part II.

[78] Ibid.

[79] Perentas Ekonomi Zaman (PEZ), no publication details, p. 57.

[80] Ibid., p. 53.

[81] Ibid., p. 13.

[82] Ibid., p. 15.

24

that disadvantage consumers in industries like telecommunications and banking, as well as protectionist policies that only benefit vested interests",[83] and terminate "backroom deals that have allowed politically linked corporate interest to reap vast and disproportionate profits at the expense of working Malaysians".[84] Fourth, he finished with NEP as UMNO practised it.[85] The distribution of economic benefit carried out in the name of NEP was unjust: "the lion's share has been cornered by the ruling elite in the guise of special bumiputra shares, contracts and privatization deals that are channelled to well-connected parties".[86] Consequently, "upward mobility has not disseminated equally throughout the rank-and-file of ordinary bumiputras" and "there is now worsening disparity and despair among the disenfranchised and underprivileged lower classes".[87] He would "rewrit[e] our affirmative action programme",[88] to assist "rank-and-file ... bumiputras", and "disenfranchised and underprivileged lower classes";[89] "the poor and underprivileged regardless of race and religion, whether ... the Tamil labourer on the plantation, the small-town Chinese shopkeeper or the Malay farmer";[90] in other words, "the masses—Malay, Chinese and Indian brethren".[91]

---

[83] PKR, *A New Dawn for Malaysia*, Part II.

[84] Ibid., Part III.

[85] Interestingly Razaleigh once said that the NEP, "defunct and ... no longer an official government policy [after] 1991" was "brought back in its afterlife as a slogan by the leadership of UMNO Youth in 2004" and remained "the most low-cost way to portray oneself as a Malay champion" (Tengku Razaleigh Hamzah, Speech at the Launch of the 2nd edition of *No Cowardly Past: James Puthucheary, Writings, Poems, Commentaries*, PJ Civic Centre, Petaling Jaya, Selangor, 22 March 2010).

[86] MEA, p. 2.

[87] Ibid.

[88] Ibid. p. 7.

[89] Ibid., p. 2.

[90] Ibid., p. 8.

[91] Ibid.

Anwar's reform agenda had a radical core that transcended Harapan's specific campaign promises.[92] A year after GE14, a freed Anwar reaffirmed his commitment to combatting social injustice, economic inequality and ethnic discrimination. He would "be progressive in identifying the right policy regime that maximizes sustainability and distributive justice".[93] "Non-discrimination is central to the position that my party takes in promoting justice,"[94] he said, pledging "to demonstrate that affirmative-action policies can be premised on need … poverty and lack of opportunity, not race or religion".[95] He rejected "governance which serves only the interests of cronies and relatives and the political elite [and] turns a deaf ear to demands for social justice".[96] His years in prison had sharpened the populist anti-elite edge of Anwar's reform agenda. Each major point of reform contained an implicit threat to those whom he called by various terms—oligarchy, ruling elite, opulent clique, or cronies.[97]

But Mahathir, the original target of *Reformasi*, was not about to morph into its spearhead. He and his elite splinter had not abandoned Najib's UMNO to overturn the social order they ruled before. Mahathir's anti-Najib campaign stressed three points. First, the kleptocrats had plundered the nation's resources and brought its finances close to breaking point. Second, the "thieves and pirates" had taken enormous debt that had to be paid by the GST, thus burdening daily life. Third, they had disgracefully lowered Malaysia from its former status as one of Southeast Asia's "tiger economies".

To hardened dissidents, the kleptocracy *was* a "legacy of Mahathirism". Mahathir, however, personalized kleptocracy, diagnosing it as Najib's failing, abetted by his co-conspirators, such as Jho Low,

---

[92] Those included the abolition of highway tolls, student debt forgiveness, and the withdrawal of the Good and Services Tax (GST).

[93] Anwar Ibrahim, "Confronting Authoritarianism", Fifteenth Annual Seymour Martin Lipset Lecture, *Journal of Democracy* 30, no. 2 (April 2019), p. 8.

[94] It is unclear if "my party" meant PKR or Harapan.

[95] Anwar, "Confronting Authoritarianism", pp. 8–9.

[96] Ibid., p. 8.

[97] Anwar used these terms interchangeably.

a corrupted UMNO and a politicized bureaucracy. Mahathir's intention was to treat the worst symptoms of kleptocracy, institute damage control, review some controversial projects, and selectively implement elements of the Harapan election manifesto. In the early days of the new government, public goodwill towards Mahathir was "magical",[98] which he could have tapped to launch major reforms. There was tremendous public approval of the seizure of the *Equanimity*, the confiscation of the luxury possessions of Rosmah Mansor, and the prosecution of Najib, Rosmah, Ahmad Zahid Hamidi, and other UMNO leaders on charges of corruption. Likewise, the renegotiation of the East Coast Railway Line, the cancellation of the Sabah pipeline, and review of the Forest City project, were welcomed as proof of a new trend of accountable governance. Those measures were necessary but they were not part of a unified agenda to "replace the damned system" as Nurul Izzah Anwar demanded. Mahathir had his excuses: his government was new, his ministers were raw, the bureaucracy was corrupt, and no one could fulfil all election promises. Without a focus on improving the lives of plebeian masses, though, a socially diverse electorate was distracted by ethnic and religious provocations pushed by those who had lost the election.

How little an oligarchic vision had in common with a plebeian agenda. For example, Mahathir pondered a "third national car" project as if it could recover his "tiger economy" glory.[99] But back in 2008 Anwar had squelched any such nostalgia by warning that "if we continue along the same path, our descendants will inherit a fourth-class economy and a divided nation".[100] With its historic electoral triumph, an insurgent electorate had reason to expect Harapan to practise Anwar's plebeian reformism. When Anwar became prime minister, could he firmly move

---

[98] Thomas, *My Story*, p. 489.

[99] Mahathir "adhered to the agenda of cleaning up corruption and I do not doubt his sincerity but I don't think he was able to put in place a systemic approach towards the goal. The most difficult conversation with [him] was what to do to change the economy. His ideas about a low-wage export-led economy were clearly outdated" (Liew Chin Tong, private communication, 15 May 2021).

[100] PKR, *A New Dawn for Malaysia*, Part II.

his reform agenda? Or would he make substantial compromises, as yet unforeseen, with the targets of a two-decade reformist struggle?

Therein lay the rub: *if* he became prime minister …

Anwar's policy disagreements with Mahathir once turned irreconcilable during a crisis. Their reform intentions could be just as divergent at a moment of triumph. At each instance, Mahathir rejected reforms that endangered the primacy of the elites.[101] And to do that, the "7th Prime Minister" would forestall a transition to Anwar as the "8th Prime Minister". In the considered opinion of Tommy Thomas, "countless statements and actions of Tun [Mahathir] indicate his refusal to honour the electoral pledge of May 2018 that Anwar would take over from him.[102]

IV.6. The Betrayal of the Elites

Despite the Harapan transition agreement, Mahathir in power was known to say that he would go "when the time came", without specifying a time. He added that it was Anwar's burden to garner sufficient support to succeed him. Such ambiguity fuelled tension within Harapan over the transition. Mahathir's partisans urged that he should serve the full Harapan term, while Anwar's loyalists wanted a clear transition date. At hand to exploit the confusion were UMNO and PAS who affected to offer Mahathir their conditional support.[103]

---

[101] Compare the argument here with this view: "from the beginning Mahathir felt that he could not depend on the Pakatan Harapan to safeguard and complete his lifetime project of creating and nurturing the Malay bourgeoisie. He needed to pass the government to a Malay majority government which would be committed to continuing the 'Malay Agenda'. This is why he brought in MPs from UMNO to bolster Bersatu, and why he cozied up with UMNO and PAS" (Jeyakumar, "The Meltdown of Pakatan Harapan").

[102] "Perhaps the coldest cut was Tun's announcement that Shafie Apdal should be the PH [Harapan] candidate for Prime Minister" (Thomas, *My Story*, p. 497).

[103] See *Sarawak Report*, "Hadi Admits There Was a Plot—Congratulates Himself on 'Bloodless Coup'", 8 March 2021, https://www.sarawakreport.org/2021/03/hadi-admits-there-was-a-plot-congratulates-himself-on-bloodless-coup/ (accessed 6 June 2021).

Mahathir's reluctance to fix a date for the Harapan transition was a replay of his old tactic. In late 1996 he declined to say when he would make way for his "anointed successor":

> Why should I give a clear timetable? The moment you give a timetable, you are a lame duck.[104] That's what happens to Western leaders.... No, I have given nothing. I have said nothing. I can go any time now or 10 years later or whatever. Depends on what the situation is like. I told you whoever is in place as my deputy will succeed me.[105]

And as late as 21 February 2021, when "nothing could hold back the forces" bent on dismantling the Harapan plan, Mahathir would only agree on "a transition to Anwar albeit without a date specified".[106] That effectively repeated what Mahathir said in December 1996, that is, Anwar would "step into the job if for some reason I should drop dead or become disabled".[107]

The failure of the second Mahathir-Anwar transition recapitulated the dynamic of political succession that derailed the first transition. When Mahathir sacked Anwar, he defied the "party at large" and reimposed the leader's prerogative to pick his successor. Najib reenacted that bit of UMNO history when he sacked Muhyiddin on 28 July 2015, not waiting for his deputy to organize a rebellion against him as Muhyiddin did against Abdullah in 2009. In February 2020 Mahathir moved to abrogate the Harapan transition agreement. He resigned as prime minister,

---

[104] This was a lame argument. The prime minister retained strong executive powers (Thomas, *My Story*, p. 494) and, in Mahathir's case, personalized the power (In-Won Hwang, *Personalized Politics: The Malaysian State Under Mahathir* [Singapore: Institute of Southeast Asian Studies, 2003].) He was no lame duck when he continued in office for sixteen months after announcing his resignation on 22 June 2002.

[105] V.G. Kulkarni, Murray Hiebert, and S. Jayasankaran, "Tough Talk", *Far Eastern Economic Review*, 24 October 1996, p. 23.

[106] Liew Chin Tiong, *Lim Kit Siang: Patriot. Leader. Fighter* (Kuala Lumpur: REFSA, 2021), p. 250.

[107] *Time*, 9 December 1996, p. 28.

requested the King to revoke the appointments of all his Cabinet members, and sought to be appointed Interim Prime Minister with the idea of forming a new government as he pleased.[108] Had he had his wish, Mahathir would become the "8th Prime Minister", beholden to no party, coalition, or, ultimately, electorate. His plan failed: he was no longer the feared wielder of state power that he was in 1998. Then Anwar tried to form a new government. But Harapan's parliamentary representation was diminished by the defection of PKR Deputy President Azmin Ali and a group of Bersatu's MPs, and the defection of Muhyiddin and the majority of the party's MPs. Soon after, the two bands of defectors, against Mahathir's will,[109] formed an ad hoc coalition with UMNO and PAS. In a confused situation with no side being required to establish publicly a majority in Parliament, Muhyiddin was appointed the "8th Prime Minister".

The dynamic of succession strife that engulfed the second transition was complicated by PKR's internal problems. Azmin was a loyal deputy to Anwar throughout the *Reformasi* period and Anwar's first term in jail. Many in and out of PKR credited Azmin with building up PKR's strength as a party. A rift opened up between the two men when Azmin became Menteri Besar of Selangor just before Anwar was imprisoned again. Subsequently, their relationship was irreparably damaged for reasons probably known only to a select group of PKR insiders. The crux is, Anwar and Azmin failed to work out a leadership transition any better than Mahathir and Anwar did. Evidently, Azmin tried to join Muhyiddin to offer a "Muhyiddin-Azmin pair" as Harapan's candidate prime minister and deputy prime minister before Harapan decided on its top leadership line-up.[110] After GE14, Anwar used his prerogative as PKR leader to curb Azmin when the latter revealed the depth of his strength

---

[108] These were "three bizarre decisions" (Thomas, *My Story*, pp. 470–73). The King "proceeded to act constitutionally by wanting to appoint [Deputy Prime Minister] Wan Azizah as ... Interim Prime Minister. Tun Mahathir put forward his own name" (ibid., p. 472).

[109] Muhyiddin and his group wanted to collaborate with UMNO as a party. Mahathir would only accept individual UMNO MPs.

[110] See Liew, *Lim Kit Siang*, pp. 221–23.

within the party. Quite simply, each man would have felt betrayed by the other. Perhaps Anwar should have retained Azmin's loyalty via a PKR succession plan because a united PKR could stiffen Harapan's spine against potential defection. Perhaps Azmin and his band, who included staunch *Reformasi* pioneers, should not have torn an electoral mandate earned by twenty years of popular struggle. Such, though, are no more than wistful reflections on lost chances.

In a sense, Muhyiddin was the logical leader for a "backdoor government" of defectors and losers. The 1MDB crisis and Najib's insecurity made Muhyiddin another "anointed successor" done out of his turn. He would have become prime minister if Najib were forced out of office. When Bersatu joined Harapan, Muhyiddin fancied his chances of being the coalition's candidate for prime minister but his hopes were swept aside by the "Mahathir-Anwar ticket".[111] Muhyiddin belonged with the Bersatu MPs who had defected from UMNO before or after GE14 only to defect from Harapan.[112] They had least interest in the reform agenda for which the "old" opposition had made sacrifices.

In short, the divides over the reform agenda and leadership succession revealed that Mahathir was not alone in wanting to shut out Anwar. Muhyiddin and Azmin rose against Mahathir *and* Harapan *and* Anwar. As the Harapan government collapsed, his second denial of Anwar proved Mahathir to be dispensable, deserted by others who did not want Anwar but had no more use for Mahathir.

V. BEYOND TRANSITIONS

Failed transitions of leadership, presumably passionate affairs for their protagonists, are only comprehensible within their social milieu and historical period. Thus, the failures of two Mahathir-Anwar transitions bear important implications beyond their personal fortunes.

---

[111] Ibid., p. 222.

[112] UMNO called its defectors "traitors". Thomas calls them "saboteurs" and "fifth columnists" whom Mahathir welcomed to Bersatu in "flagrant violation of electoral promises" (Thomas, *My Story*, p. 499).

V.1. Dysfunctional Succession

The first consequence is the obvious one of continuing disorder in political succession. A smooth transition permits manageable shifts in generational terms, policy directions, and the demarcation of new social concerns. Here is a balanced sense of what a shift from "Mahathir's vision" to "Anwar's renaissance" might have signified: "many of us admired the pugnacity of Mahathir and his technological ambitions, and shared in his nationalism and in the goals of Vision 2020 [but] were discomfited by the obsession with economics and winced not a little at his outbursts against 'the west'". Anwar symbolized a "dream beyond that of economics": "a dream of a civic and civil society, taking its place as an equal in the community of nations, able to absorb the good that others have to offer us, without losing our distinctive character … confident enough in itself to undertake a fruitful cultural exchange with the rest of the world."[113] Before 1997, it looked as if a change from Mahathir to Anwar would allow those shifts to take place as the century ended. By persecuting his heir apparent, Mahathir set off unsatisfactory changes of leadership. He was followed by Abdullah, for whom he had contempt, while he impatiently pushed for Najib in whom he placed groundless hopes. From a longer perspective, the unrealized transitions may be traced to a dynamic of dysfunctional succession that began in UMNO, as the fates of UMNO's pretenders proved: Razaleigh was beaten by Musa who was defeated by Ghafar who was pushed off by Anwar who was sacked by Mahathir and replaced by Abdullah who was ousted by Muhyiddin who was purged by Najib. Under Mahathir, UMNO was split in 1987. Under Najib, the party's dominance ended ingloriously. To date, Muhyiddin, as head of PN, had not appointed a deputy prime minister, a sure sign of dysfunctional succession.[114]

---

[113] Khoo, "Thinking the Unthinkable", p. 7.

[114] On 7 July 2021, as this manuscript was ready for printing, the Prime Minister's Office announced the appointment, with immediate effect, of Ismail Sabri Yaakob as the Deputy Prime Minister.

V.2. Social Divides and Reform Agenda

The second consequence is the setback suffered by the "reform agenda". For better or worse, the agenda which Anwar articulated grew out of a social divide exemplified by the career trajectories of Mahathir, Daim and Anwar. The "humane economy", as Anwar called his reformist vision, targeted issues of inequality, corruption, economic resilience, and cultural restiveness. Anwar had not based his politics on subaltern discontent before he fell. After all, the protests in his defence crafted dissident narratives of electoral, judicial, social and political reform that allowed many streams of discontent to converge as a powerful movement of multiethnic socially inclusive opposition. This movement saw its historic victory betrayed by the second unrealized transition. The movement control orders imposed because of the COVID-19 pandemic, and the continued suspension of Parliament under a declaration of Emergency, check a tense and unforgiving stance towards the "government without an electoral mandate". The first failed transition sparked a two-decade subaltern revolt. The second failed transition disrupted a much-awaited project of reform that is bound to resurface when the pandemic fades if its dire economic impact exerts more pressure on an unreformed system. The twenty-year *Reformasi* will "not go gentle into that good night".

V.3. Malaise of the Malay Political Class

The general malaise of the Malay political class, the third consequence of the unrealized transitions, emerged directly from the demoralization of the class after the financial crisis of 1997 and the Anwar crisis of 1998. The malaise, elsewhere depicted as the "parlous condition of Malay politics",[115] persisted under the Abdullah and Najib regimes. The Harapan regime had the best chance of the time to supply an antidote of fresh national vision, deeper social understanding, and strong commitment

---

[115] Khoo Boo Teik, *Malay Politics: Parlous Condition, Persistent Problems,* Trends in Southeast Asia, no. 17/2020 (Singapore: ISEAS – Yusof Ishak Institute, 2020).

to reform. Muhyiddin's coalition, Perikatan Nasional (PN, or National Alliance), burdened by questionable legitimacy, aggravates the disorder of Malay politics. The PN was formed as an anti-Anwar front consisting of ex-UMNO and UMNO politicians whom Anwar fought over two decades, *Reformasi* stalwarts who fell out with Anwar as PKR's own factionalism went out of control, and PAS conservatives whose Islamism never found favour with Anwar. The PN's parties and politicians portray themselves as a "Malay-Muslim Front" of *Malay* parties and *Malay* politicians on a mission to preserve *Malay* dominance. But their fixation on "Malay-ness" will not resolve the deep intra-Malay conflicts that characterized the subaltern struggles bearing the names of *Reformasi*, Pakatan Rakyat, and Harapan.[116] Anwar mocked at that fixation as mere diversion. Whenever UMNO leaders were challenged over corruption and social injustice, he said, they would shout *Hidup Melayu!* (Long live the Malays!).

V.4. Mahathir's Final Failure

Mahathir has long held a saviour's view of himself and his place in Malaysian politics.[117] He claims to have honed his training in medicine into lifelong skills of diagnosing, treating, healing, and saving the body politick.[118] At the juncture of 2015–16, Mahathir spoke of saving the country urgently. He was not the only person to say so for there was a nationwide *Save Malaysia* campaign then. For a variety of reasons, many people took him at his word. Even so, a sceptic might have observed that it was not the country alone that needed rescuing. Surely Mahathir had to redeem himself from the ignominy of his persecution of Anwar, the scorn that Malays had for *Mahafiraun*, the blame for the "collusion,

---

[116] For example, one of the emblems of "Malay-ness", the NEP, "has been reinvented as an inalienable platform of a Malay Agenda that at one and the same time asserts Malay supremacy and perpetuates the myth of Malay dependency" (Razaleigh, Speech at the Launch of the 2nd edition of *No Cowardly Past*).

[117] Khoo Boo Teik, "Once Mahathir, Always Mahathir?", *Malaysiakini*, 18 April 2018, https://www.malaysiakini.com/news/420334.

[118] Khoo Boo Teik, "Dr Mahathir Dissects Kleptocracy", *Malaysiakini*, 16 April 2018, https://www.malaysiakini.com/news/420048.

corruption and nepotism" that linked his era to kleptocracy, and the blunder of favouring Najib for prime minister for no better reason than to repay Mahathir's debt to Najib's father, Razak.[119] Rarely in Malaysian politics had anyone had to save himself more than Mahathir. Rarely did someone so ignobly squander his chance to do so. One result of the unrealized transitions must simply be a final stamp of failure on "Mahathir's legacy".

V.5. The Spectre of Anwar

The final consequence concerns Anwar. Throughout his career he was commonly characterized as a charismatic and a "chameleon". As the first, he drew many people to him; as the second he repelled some of them. Most people overlook a third characterization, now retrieved by the unrealized transitions. Anwar has been a *spectre* haunting the consciousness of many people. Those include his political rivals, of course, but also the police, judges, senior bureaucrats, corporate figures, and media bosses who had a hand in bringing him down. Anwar may be twice loser in political succession. But whatever the public polls say of his present popularity, he has not been vanquished. He has outlived Mahathir twice, so to speak—returning to politics after the latter retired, and retaining substantial support compared with Mahathir's current negligible presence. Anwar remains a contender who causes much anxiety for the regime. There are criticisms of his "obsession" with being prime minister.[120] Some are raised by people who want Anwar to

---

[119] Years before Mahathir decided that Najib was unsuitable, someone asked, "The elite begets the elite? ... So, Najib was chosen all along because he is assumed to inherit all the wonders of Tun Razak?" (Sakmongkol AK47, "The Vicious Cycle of Malaysian Politics", 25 December 2008, http://sakmongkol.blogspot.com/2008/12/vicious-cycle-of-malaysian-politics.html [accessed 26 January 2012].)

[120] Various views of Anwar on this matter are discussed in Tashny Sukumaran and Bhavan Jaipragas, "The Nearly Man: Will Anwar Ibrahim Ever Lead Malaysia?", *South China Morning Post*, 5 December 2020, https://www.scmp.com/week-asia/politics/article/3112661/nearly-man-will-anwar-ibrahim-ever-lead-malaysia (accessed 14 June 2021).

focus on leading the opposition at a difficult time. Other criticisms are issued by his detractors who wish to invalidate his claim on succession in order to legitimize the PN regime. For his opponents in the latter group, there is a companion obsession *with* Anwar. They obsessively fear his becoming the prime minister. He might wreak vengeance on those who had caused him much misery for a long time. He still sees himself as the nemesis of the "the top billionaires and the political elite" who say, "At all costs, anybody else but Anwar. Why? Am I racist or a religious bigot or corrupt? No ... because they think I'm too dangerous because I will have to use every power in my authority to stop the excesses."[121] Is he genuine or delusional here? Without a realized transition, who knows? For now, it must be assumed that a charismatic and chameleonic Anwar has not lost his talent for staying relevant to the time, milieu, and hopes of the plebeian classes. If conditions cause those classes to rise again, Anwar may appear to them not as a spectre but as "one of us".

Acknowledgement

I wish to thank ISEAS – Yusof Ishak Institute for my Visiting Senior Fellowship which gave me an excellent opportunity to write on contemporary Malaysian politics. In this regard, I am grateful to Francis Hutchinson, Lee Hwok Aun, Norshahril Saat, and the staff of ISEAS – Yusof Ishak Institute for their kind assistance. Francis, Hwok Aun, and Fong Chin Wei offered many suggestions that helped me revise a draft of this essay. I would like to thank Abdul Rahman Embong, Chia Kwang Chye, Jomo K. S., Guanie Lim, Liew Chin Tong, Mustafa K. Anuar, Toh Kin Woon, Yeap Jin Soo, and Zaharom Nain whose views in private communication deepened my understanding of an era in flux.

---

[121] Anwar Ibrahim, quoted in Azeem Ibrahim, "Will It Ever Be Anwar's Turn?", *FP*, 28 March 2021, https://foreignpolicy.com/2021/03/28/anwar-ibrahim-malaysia-opposition-pm/ (accessed 14 June 2021).